AF592879

BRITAIN IN OLD PHOTOGRAPHS

LEICESTERSHIRE PEOPLE

R.P. JENKINS

SUTTON PUBLISHING LIMITED

Sutton Publishing Limited
Phoenix Mill · Thrupp · Stroud
Gloucestershire · GL5 2BU

First published 1996

Copyright © R.P. Jenkins, 1996

British Library Cataloguing in Publication Data
A catalogue record for this book is available from the British Library.

ISBN 0-7509-1275-8

Typeset in 10/12 Perpetua.
Typesetting and origination by
Sutton Publishing Limited.
Printed in Great Britain by
Ebenezer Baylis, Worcester.

To Jess

Contents

Comfortable in reefer jacket and nautical cap, the Rev. J.P.A. Fletcher relaxes with members of his family at Burbage Rectory, *c.* 1910.

INTRODUCTION

This book is about Leicestershire people. It is not only about famous or wealthy Leicestershire people – though there are some of them in it – it is about all Leicestershire people. It is not so much about what they did, or said, or even what was done to them (though you'll find some of that); it is about what they looked like. This, for want of a better description, is a 'family album' for Leicestershire.

This photographic survey draws almost exclusively – save only for a few images in the possession of the author – from the extensive photographic collections of the Leicestershire Museums, Arts and Records Service. Those collections include photographs from virtually every parish in Leicestershire and record almost every activity of the county's people. Future books may deal with the county's work, recreation and its involvement in war; this one is concerned with how the people of Leicestershire appeared – both to themselves and to others.

The story does not begin with the invention of photographs of course, because for centuries before Leicestershire people appeared in drawings, in sculptured or incised funerary monuments and other carvings, and painted on glass. Many of these depictions are not portraits but they nevertheless do portray Leicestershire 'types' or 'ideals' and are of interest for that reason.

From 1839 (and the birth of the Daguerreotype – the first practical photographic process) portraiture changed. From that date we see the people of Leicestershire as they were. It is true that photography remained a ponderous affair, with heavy cameras, glass negatives and slow exposure times. Photographs had to be carefully 'composed' and 'sitters' kept still but this had its advantages – as many of the photographs here show. Photography became a serious business and people were content to wait while the photographer ensured the survival of their appearance for all time.

This reverence for photography lasted long after Eastman's invention of the 'Kodak' camera, with its roll of celluloid film, made action shots possible. We still experience a trace of it in the photographer's studio or with wedding 'groups'. Press photography, which blossomed after the First World War and which provides many of the images in the final section of this book, continues to fulfil its traditional role of recording formal scenes of people and their activities.

The photographs that follow have been chosen with care. They have been chosen because they are technically good, or because they have a story to tell. For each one reproduced here there are many others that would have done as well in creating a portrait of the county: a thousand years of Leicestershire People.

There can be few Leicestershire 'portraits' earlier than this one, tucked carefully away beside the vestry at St Peter's, Church Langton. Possibly a thousand years old he is older than the church by several centuries and may even have Pagan roots. The figure is crude – and may have been even cruder at one time!

SECTION ONE

BEFORE THE PORTRAIT (*c*.1000–1600)

Before photography there are no wholly reliable likenesses. Some artists – Holbein is perhaps the obvious example – could capture the character of their subjects but we can never be sure that we see a man as he really was. Only in sculpture do we perhaps have an advantage as we see the fully rounded form. Few effigies before 1600 are likely to be portraits but do we see in the images that follow some inkling of a 'Leicestershire face'?

The stone effigy of Sir John de Digby at Tilton on the Hill. After more than 700 years it is still possible to discern individual links of his mail armour.

A fourteenth-century figure from the stained-glass at Coston.

The fate of gossips in Leicestershire! A medieval wall painting uncovered in 1869 above one of the pillars of the aisle at Scalford parish church.

Two heads for the price of one! Whose are the faces on these capitals of the chancel arch of St Catherine's, Burbage?

The parish church at Lutterworth has many claims to fame. Its medieval wall-paintings are justly admired. Here a pair of figures 'burst through' the later depiction of a King; one of three from the famous moral tale of three monarchs who met their own corpses while hunting and so learned the nearness of mortality!

Too good to be true? This unknown lady from St Mary's, Melton Mowbray, with two angels beside her pillow, was carved in about 1400 but can she have survived nearly six centuries so perfectly unscathed?

Unusually, this big-mouth serves a useful purpose. One of several bizarre or grotesque carvings on the church at Tilton, this gargoyle throws the rainwater that might otherwise harm the fabric of the building far away into the churchyard.

Needing only a visor to complete his plate armour (though how he would fit his moustache inside it is unclear) lies the effigy of Sir John Blacket at Idbury, Oxfordshire. Not a Leicestershire man at all, he nevertheless represented the county in the Parliaments of 1409 and 1410, 1414 and 1420.

The brass to Geoffrey Sherard, Esq., at Stapleford. Although the brass was made in his lifetime (about 1490) it is unlikely to be a portrait. It is probable, too, that Sherard never wore the full plate armour we see him in today.

The enigmatic smile of Elizabeth, the wife of John Southill who died in 1493, commemorated in brass at Stockerston.

The original 'woolly-backs'? Two Woodwoses – or wild men (though one is of course a woman!) from the monument at Ashby Folville to Ralph Woodford who died in 1498.

Fragments of the medieval glass at Loddington church show a bishop with mitre and staff – but who is he? A saint or the donor of the glass?

This crippled bedesman at Lockington has been mourning on the tomb of Elizabeth the wife of John, Baron Ferrers of Chartley for nearly 500 years. Less than a foot tall, he shows perfectly the skill of the alabaster carvers and the detail they could produce in such tiny spaces.

Is this the stern face of a local man staring out from the early sixteenth-century pews at Croxton Kerrial?

The effigy in St Margaret's, Leicester, of John Penny, once Abbot of Leicester, who died in 1520 as Bishop of Carlisle.

The heavy jowls of Bishop John Penny. It seems likely that this lifesize effigy in alabaster was erected in Penny's lifetime – perhaps while he was still Abbot of Leicester as the robes of abbot and bishop are so alike – and may therefore be a portrait of the Tudor cleric.

The Rev. Walter Savage died on 24 May 1518. At the time of his death he had been the rector of Stretton en le Field – which he knew as a parish of Derbyshire but which from 1897 has been in Leicestershire – for some thirty-three years. Savage's head rests on a tasselled pillow beside which are the 'tools of his trade'; his chalice and clasped missal or mass book. He wears the decorated vestments of a priest from before the Reformation and creation of a Protestant Church of England.

Robert Scales, once vicar of Lockington, who died in 1540. His will contains many interesting bequests including that of a cow named Hemington to his servant, Margaret Carter.

Thomas Malle (d. 1545) and his wife, also of Lockington. They too benefited from Robert Scales' generosity; he left them a malt mill 'as an yer lome' (heirloom).

The faces of Robert Nundy and his wives Elizabeth and Alice have been staring out at us from their alabaster slab for some 460 years. Nundy died in April 1526 and was buried in his parish church at Ashby de la Zouch. His slab lay undiscovered under the pews of the church until 1829 but is now displayed at the west end of the church, safe from erosion by the feet of passers-by.

A Leicestershire burial of about 1520, originally from the windows of 18 Highcross Street, Leicester. Prayers are said for the soul of the departed, whose body in its shroud – but no coffin – is lowered into the grave.

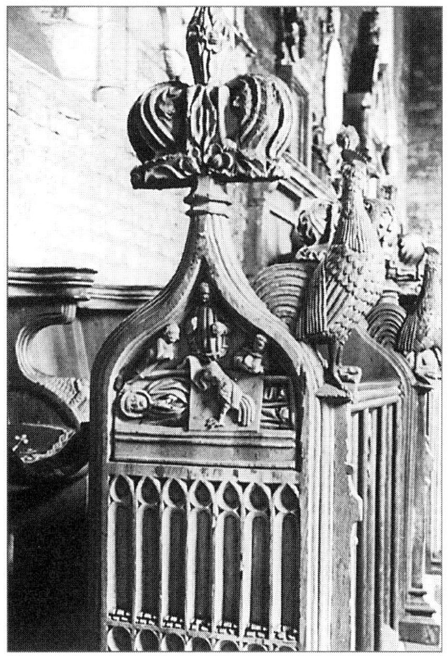

Burial and resurrection at Noseley. The ornate fifteenth-century stall at the Chapel of the Hazleriggs shows a burial – with the corpse in its shroud and coffin and the priest above – but the crowing cock brings hope of eternal life.

The tomb at Fenny Drayton to Nicholas Purefoy who died in 1543 and to his wife Jane has beautifully carved figures of their children at its side. Here are George and Ralph Purefoy dressed according to their stations in Tudor society. The beads at Ralph's belt would not survive the religious changes of Edward VI's reign. The sculpture is almost certainly by Richard Parker who made the monument below in the same year.

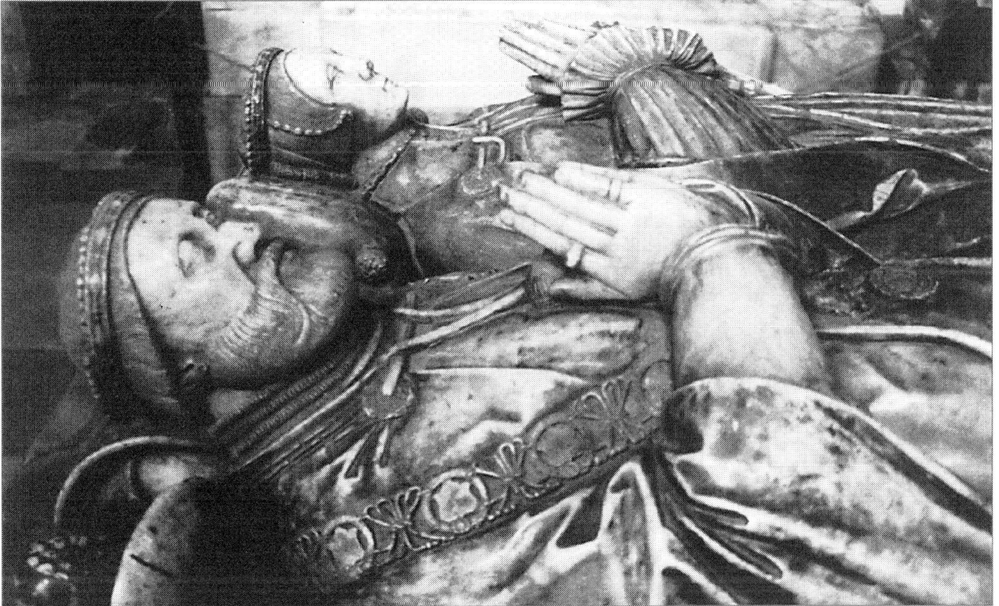

The effigies of Thomas Manners, 1st Earl of Rutland and his Countess, Eleanor Paston, beautifully sculptured from Staffordshire alabaster by Richard Parker of Burton-on-Trent. Parker was paid £20 for his work in 1544.

The face of Jane Warburton, the wife of Sir William Turville who died in 1549, from their monument in the church at Aston Flamville. The features are striking but it is not a portrait.

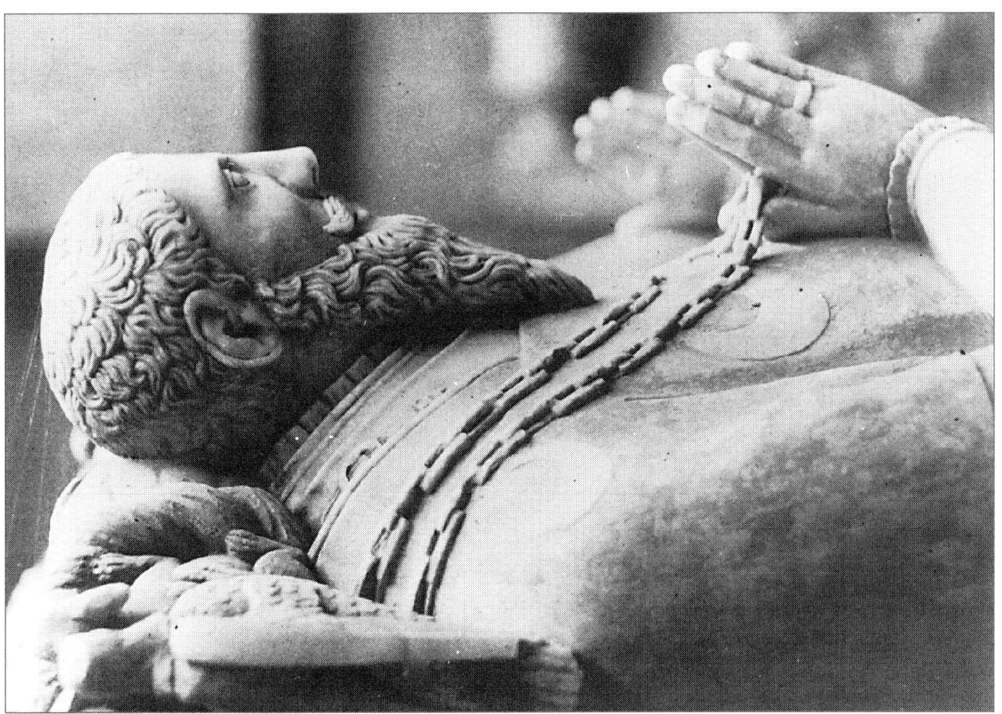

The effigy, at Stoughton, of Thomas Farnham who died in 1562. The crispness of the carving is due to the re-cutting by Peter Scheemakers in 1739.

One of the finest of Leicestershire's many incised slabs, this commemorates Ralph Leeson of Packington (who died in 1587) and his wives, Elizabeth and Ursula. Though not portraits, the images show perfectly the clothing worn by provincial Elizabethan gentry.

Robert Herrick may be 'dead and rotten' but he is still remembered for his charity and for his service as MP for the borough of Leicester in 1588 and as its mayor in 1584, 1593 and 1605.

The 1590s memorial in brass to Thomas and Cornelia Duport at Shepshed. The engraver, probably in the workshop of Gerard Johnson at Southwark, followed the tradition of placing sons behind their father and daughters behind their mother as they kneel at prayer.

The stern visage of Edmund Brudenell (d. 1590) at Stonton Wyville. His monument records him as 'a lover of hospitality, pitiful to the Poor, a quieter of contraversies in his countrie, beloved by his neighbours . . .'.

Once on his tomb, this brass to the Rev. William Heathcote, who died in 1594, is now fixed to the wall of his church at Aylestone. Like the priests on pages 17 and 18 Heathcote has his book but his plain robes are those of the Protestant faith.

Kneeling alongside her parents' tomb at Bottesford is this figure of Frances, the daughter of John, 4th Earl of Rutland and Countess Elizabeth. She married William, Lord Willoughby of Parham, in 1603.

A fascinating glimpse at the back of an Elizabethan gentleman. Every detail of Roger Manners' armour and its fastenings is clear in this splendid piece of carving by Gerard Johnson of Southwark. Like the figures above and overleaf it forms only a tiny part of the monument.

Roger Manners, later 5th Earl of Rutland, kneeling in prayer at the side of his parents' tomb in Bottesford church. Ten years after the figure was made, in 1601, Roger was implicated in the revolt of the Earl of Essex against Elizabeth I. Imprisoned in the Tower he was released only after paying a fine of £10,000.

SECTION TWO

BEFORE THE PHOTOGRAPH (1600–1850)

Whether true or not, Oliver Cromwell's famous desire to be painted 'warts and all', represents two important developments of this period; the desire for recognisable portraiture and the ability of the artist to provide it. There is an individuality in funerary sculpture and painted portraits that promises us some idea of the subjects real appearance however idealised or stylised it may be. We see the people of Leicestershire in clothes they might have worn and there is a hope that we might know them if we chanced to meet them.

The monument to Augustin and Anne Nichols at Tilton on the Hill. Although Augustin died in 1638 the sculptor of his monument chose to depict his family much as Gerard Johnson had shown the Duports fifty years before (see page 24). Two sons who died in infancy are shown behind their father wrapped in their chrysom cloth 'shrouds'. The figures still retain traces of their original paint, indicating how colourful the monument must originally have been.

Mary Bond, the mother of Robert Herrick, at the age of 90 (in 1604). Mary died in 1611 surrounded, according to her epitaph in St Martin's, Leicester, by a devoted family of 142 children, grandchildren and great-grandchildren.

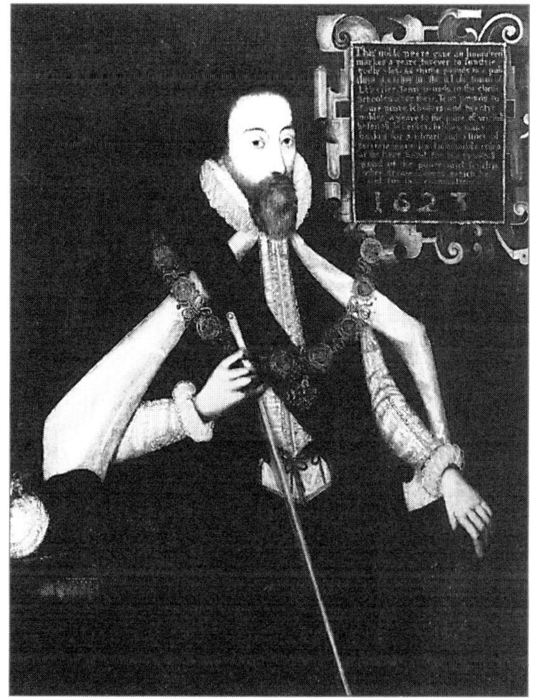

Leicester Corporation paid £2 10 *s* in 1623 for this portrait of Henry Hastings, 3rd Earl of Huntingdon. Nominally Leicester's overlord, Hastings acted more as its patron and earned the thanks of the Corporation for his support in obtaining a charter from Elizabeth I. The Huntingdon Tower, a relic of Hastings' town home, survived in Leicester's High Street until 3 May 1902.

The monument to Francis Staresmore, who died in 1626, at Frowlesworth. Below the effigy are figures of his children: Dorothy, Catherine, George (who died in infancy), William, John, another John (who died young), Hannah and Robert.

The face of Francis Staresmore. The streaks of iron-oxide in the alabaster disfigure his features but would originally have been hidden beneath paint.

Sir Thomas Nevill at Nevill Holt. Sir Thomas died in 1636 at the age of 81 – though his effigy, in armour he almost certainly never wore, is of a somewhat younger man.

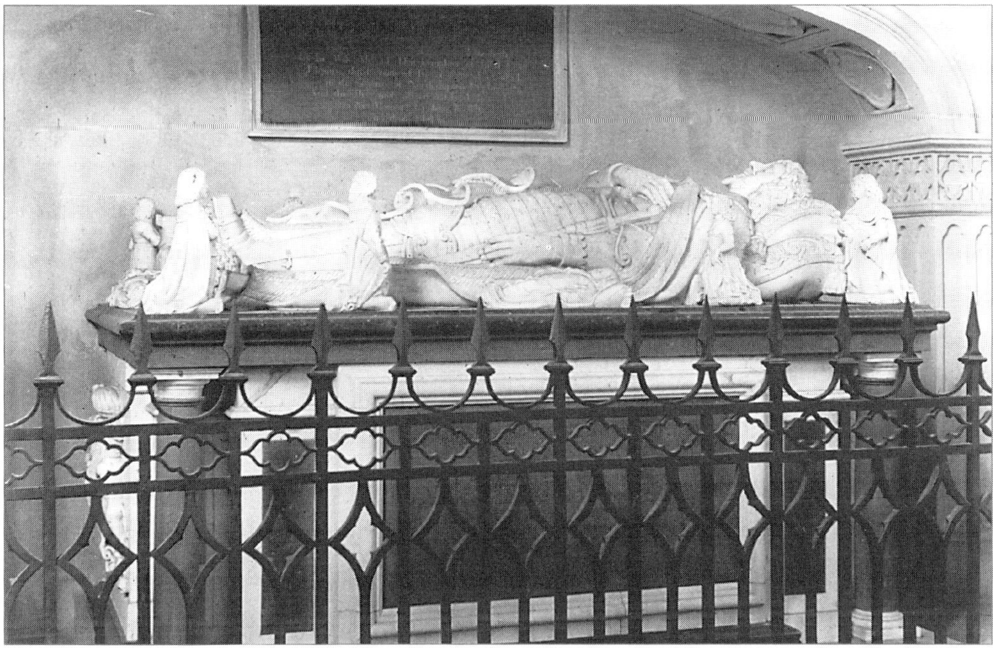

The magnificent white marble monument to William Sherard, Baron Leitrim, who died in 1640, at Stapleford. Beside Sherard lies his wife, Abigail, who paid for the tomb and diminutive figures of their children.

Sir Francis Smith of Queniborough: a tiny figure beside the tomb of his parents George and Anne Smith, at Ashby Folville. Sir Francis died in 1629 at the age of 59.

Mary Smith, literally a 'weeper' beside the tomb of her parents, George and Anne Smith of Ashby Folville (George died in 1607).

Sir Richard Halford waits resignedly on his tomb at Wistow for the Resurrection. The figure of his son Anthony – who died in 1657, a year before Sir Richard – is by his side.

The children of Sir Arthur Hazlerigg – by his two wives Frances and Dorothy. His eldest surviving son, Thomas (second in line here) had the distinction – or misfortune – of fighting in the last battle of the English Civil War. He joined with John Lambert in his ill-fated attempt to prevent the Restoration of Charles II but was captured with his troops during a skirmish near Daventry on 22 April 1660.

'Having passed the latter part of his life in the study of English history, he acquired a melancholy habit' is Nichols' curious explanation for the retiring disposition of Thomas Staveley (1626–1684), a native of East Langton.

Mary Onebye, who married Thomas Staveley in 1656. They lived together until her death, at Belgrave Vicarage, on 12 October 1669.

Sir Christopher Packe reclining in his robes as Lord Mayor of London on his tomb at Prestwold. A staunch supporter of Oliver Cromwell – who knighted hin in 1655, Packe was driven from public life at the Restoration and spent the last twenty years of his life at Cotes, near Loughborough.

Sir William and Lady Anñ Villiers, both of whom died in 1711, at Brooksby church. The life-size figures of marble are caught in a theatrical pose which matches their ornate surroundings.

The Rev. William Paul, born at Ashby Parva in 1678 and hanged, drawn and quartered at Tyburn in 1716. Paul sided with the Jacobites in 1715 but had the misfortune, on a visit to London, to run into the forces of law and order in the shape of Thomas Bird, a Leicestershire JP 'I wish I had quarters enough', declared Paul, 'to send to every parish of the kingdom, to testify that a Clergyman of the Church of England was martyred for being loyal to his King.'

Richard Hayward carved this monument to the Rev. Slaughter Clark and his wife Rachel at Theddingworth in 1772. Rachel left £360 for the work in her will (but surely cannot have intended the impression that she has fallen asleep mid sermon!).

The Rev. Andrew Burnaby (*c.* 1734–1812). In his youth Burnaby travelled widely in North America and Italy but settled down by 1767 to divide his time between Baggrave Hall and his duties as vicar of Greenwich. In 1786 he became archdeacon of Leicester.

The Rev. Joseph and Ellen Winks; a typical pair of early Victorian portraits. Although the Rev. Joseph Fowkes Winks was a native of Gainsborough in Lincolnshire, he occupied a key place in the religious and political life of Leicester from the 1830s. Winks had three parallel careers; as a Baptist minister, a pioneering journalist and as a reforming member of the Corporation.

The sad figure of Charles Hussey Packe who died whilst a schoolboy at Eton in 1842. His grieving parents chose one of the foremost sculptors of the day, Richard Westmacott jnr, to capture their sadness in stone. The monument is in the church at Prestwold.

John Thomas Ward, with stick and hoop, in about 1840. His son, Thomas Charles, became managing director of the Midland Educational Company.

William Gardiner (1770–1853). A light-hearted fellow by all accounts, he played a dominant role in the intellectual life of Leicester throughout the early nineteenth century. 'Judah' was his own oratorio combining the words of the Bible and music of Beethoven.

There is much of the demagogue here in the face of John Skevington, the leader of Leicestershire's Chartists from 1838 until the early 1840s. His demands – declared in the Peoples' Charter which he clutches – seems eminently reasonable now; universal male suffrage, payment of MPs, secret voting and annual parliaments.

Thomas Paget (1778–1862) could have lived quietly at Humberstone Hall on the profits of his bank. He preferred to make the reform of Leicester's local government his mission, and when in 1835 the Municipal Corporations Act gave him victory he received the rewards of his labours and became, in January 1836, the first mayor of the reformed Corporation.

SECTION THREE

BEFORE THE SNAPSHOT (1850–1914)

It was widely thought in the 1840s that the new art of photography would kill the old one of painting. This chapter shows how wrong the view was. Photographs did not replace painting; photography accompanied it. Photographers worked as artists did, in studios with classical backdrops or carefully placed curtains and furniture. By the 1890s however the field was opening to amateurs, men like G.M. Henton and R.C. Stewart who took their cameras into the field to record everyday life. Henton's interest seems to have begun as an aid to his watercolour painting while Stewart used a well-equipped studio in his work at the County Lunatic Asylum and extended his photography to record his friends and family at home and on holiday.

The professional photographer was not left behind either. Studio and outdoor work (for new fashions like picture postcards) was developed while improvements in printing led to a new calling in photographic journalism. R.C. Stewart used photography in medical work. The police used it in the fight against crime. The 'mug-shot' was born and some are rightly included here as a Leicestershire rogues gallery.

The men responsible. . . . An outing by Leicester photographers, *c.* 1910. George White (one of the leaders of the Unemployed March in 1905, see page 82) is second from the left in the back row.

PERSONALITIES

Edward Foster was 101 years old when this photograph was taken in 1864. Born on 8 November 1762 he was a teenager when America gained her independence and lived to hear of her Civil War.

George Reeves, the clockmaker of Appleby Magna (rear left) with some of his friends and neighbours. Ann and Charles Bates with their son, Charles T. are next to Reeves on the back row while seated in front are a Mr Booton and Mrs Bates snr with her brother. The photograph is a ferrotype, a process in which the image is held on a sensitised iron plate. No negative is made and so the image is reversed (as the men's watch-chains and buttons show).

Peter Alfred Taylor MP, 1819–91. Taylor represented the Borough of Leicester in Parliament from 1862 until 1884. As a Unitarian and partner in Courtaulds it was natural that he voted with the radical wing of the Liberal party.

The *Wyvern* called it 'a face familiar to almost everyone'. This portrait of Sir Israel Hart, four times Mayor of Leicester, was painted by A.S. Cope in 1896. Hart is still remembered in Leicester as the donor of the ornate fountain in Town Hall Square.

Henry Broadhurst served as Liberal MP for Leicester from 1894 until 1906. Though generally regarded as a 'Labour leader', because of his early association with trades unions, Broadhurst's later life was characterised by disputes with the TUC over his lukewarm support for an eight-hour day and other causes.

Dress notwithstanding, this is the steady gaze of a future captain of industry; Theodore Burgess Ellis (1860–1942), director of Ellis & Everard Ltd, and of Joseph Ellis & Sons Ltd. An early studio portrait.

Theodore Burgess Ellis, *c.* 1864. Who could tell that this tired little boy would turn (forty years on) into a director of Ellis and Everard Ltd – coal, lime, corn and artificial manure merchants.

Emma Burgess, the wife of Thomas Burgess, of The Grange, Wigston. She was photographed in about 1860 in the studio of the noted Leicester photographer, John Burton.

The youthful Frederick Thompson Mott, *c.* 1860. A wine merchant by trade and a scientist by inclination, Mott is now best remembered for his studies of Charnwood Forest though they represent only a fraction of his literary and philosophical output.

Four sides to Mr Frederick Mott; all reduced to the size of a visiting-card. They represent perhaps the Gallowtree Gate wine merchant, the Liberal councillor, the scientist and the sometime president of the Leicester Literary & Philosophical Society.

Ragdale, 1896. The Frisby children show off their pets to G.M. Henton. A dog, cat and magpie all seem content to relax together in the sunshine.

Blanche Glover and some of her playmates, photographed by G.M. Henton at Witherley just after midday on 9 August 1911.

Sir Sewallis-Edward Shirley, 10th Earl Ferrers and his wife, Ina Maude, take tea in their first-floor sitting room at Staunton Harold, *c.* 1890. This elegant room has since been partitioned and is used by patients at the Sue Ryder Home which now occupies Staunton Harold Hall.

The 10th Earl Ferrers lost in the Orangery at Staunton Harold, *c.* 1890. The Earl has adopted the correct costume, of tweed Norfolk jacket and breeches, for an expedition amongst the ferns and fronds of the Orangery, now sadly demolished.

The Bown family of Claybrooke Magna, 1887. Great sadness lies behind this picture. The 1891 census returns tell us who they all are – except for the babe-in-arms. Michael Bown, Claybrooke's baker, stands with his wife Sarah and their children, left to right: Marion, Lenton, Evelyn, Lonzo and Helena. Poor Dora Alice, their baby, died in February 1888 aged 1½ years – only weeks after this picture was taken.

Harry Sharpe (aged 6) in 1904. An ordinary boy in a new collar but an old jacket. His image would probably not have survived except for a brief incident on 28 December 1903 when he fell into the canal in Leicester and was saved from drowning by Ambrose Marriott (who received half-a-guinea from the town's Bravery Fund).

John Edward Faire (1843–1929) of Evington Hall was, as his portrait suggests, a prosperous businessman. His fortune, as a director of Faire Bros & Co., elastic web manufacturers, was based on men's braces and women's underwear.

A Great Central Railway navvy lounges at the Leicestershire county boundary south of Stanford on Soar. A beautifully composed view by S.W.A. Newton, *c.* 1896.

Navvies at work on the Great Central Railway near Leicester, *c.* 1897. Another example of the professional touch of S.W.A. Newton.

When G.M. Henton saw paviours at work in Leicester in April 1890 (above) and October 1894 (below) he chose not to record their labour but rather their lunchbreaks.

Presumably a wedding group, with two bridesmaids, this typical studio photograph was inscribed ‘A Happy New Year to my daughter Donna, with love from Mother, 1912’.

Mrs Hawkins, a campaigner for women’s suffrage, is given a bouquet on her release from prison, *c.* 1914.

A pipe-smoking R.C. Stewart caught in horticultural mood by Mr Smallwood; perhaps a colleague of his at the County Asylum.

The Rev. J.H. Fry pauses in his reading to chat to his wife. A peaceful scene in the garden of the rectory at Osgathorpe, *c.* 1900.

From somewhere deep within this boiled shirt and starched collar came the beautiful baritone of Frank Hanford of 31 West Street, Southfields, Leicester. A voice moreover which had won a shield and silver medal at the 1907 Leicester YMCA Eisteddfod.

Florence Blackwell as Jill-All-Alone in the Leicester Amateur Dramatic Society's production of *Merrie England* in May 1905. 'Miss F. Blackwell', the *Leicester Guardian* declared, 'sang very prettily, as she always does.'

Mr A.J. Cooper. He retired from the General Post Office in 1912 after forty-two years' service. His medals record his long service and the coronation of George V.

Nearly a sixth of a ton of law and order – PC John William Stephens of the Leicester Borough Police. A jovial character, he could hardly be missed when on duty at the Clock Tower or Market Place. Stephens served from February 1886 until his death in May 1908.

A detachment of the Leicestershire County Police – some of the 187 men who made up the force in 1912.

An eccentric choice of headgear seems to have been the qualification for membership of Lodge 515 of the Loyal Independent Order of Caledonian Corks, photographed by H.B. Cooper of 13 Abbey Park Road, Leicester, *c.* 1910.

Nurses on duty in Ward F.3 at the County Asylum (now Leicester University), *c.* 1905. A photograph taken by Dr Rothsay C. Stewart who was Medical Superintendent there from 1895 until 1908.

Ruth's Romance, one of a number of amateur theatricals put on at the County Asylum, *c.* 1895. R.C. Stewart enters by the garden gate to interrupt Rose Fry (as Ruth) and E. Leonard.

More thespian activity, this time *Little Toddlekins* with, left to right: R. Fry, E. Leonard, J.W. Noble, M. Duff, Mrs Beaumont and a bewigged R.C. Stewart.

Guests of R.C. Stewart in the Medical Superintendent's garden at the County Asylum, *c.* 1900. The men seem prepared for cricket; the ladies ready for anything!

Possibly the day of the Royal Infirmary v County Asylum cricket match, *c.* 1900. Stewart (perching precariously on the right, having dashed round from setting his camera perhaps) gives us only the surnames of some of his colleagues, left to right: Sevestre, ?, Richards, ?, Bond, Blakesby, Douglas, Williams, Marriott, Carter, Pope, Stewart and Franklin.

Beryl Pennington and Ada Stewart captured forever by R.C. Stewart in 1896.

Beryl Pennington strums her guitar in the Medical Superintendent's garden at the Leicestershire County Asylum, *c.* 1896.

The bearded figure of Claude Douglas, Hon Surgeon at the Leicester Royal Infirmary, looms over this group at the County Asylum, *c.* 1900. R.C. Stewart is again behind the lens.

The opening of the eighteen-hole course at the Leicestershire Golf Club, 1899. Charles James Billson, the Club President, stands modestly at the centre rear having abandoned a golf club for his umbrella.

Pupils at Holy Trinity School, Leicester, 1879. On 7 November that year J.R. Blakiston, HM Inspector, visited the school and reported 'Miss Harbutt has taken great pains to overcome the weakness noted last year and to make herself familiar with the best methods of Infant teaching.'

Mrs Betty Islip, who moulded a generation of Leicester girls as headmistress of the Collegiate School from 1866 until 1884. Mrs Islip entered teaching only when her husband, the Congregations Minister at Kibworth, died. Mrs Islip herself died at the age of 76 in March 1897.

Miss Seymour, the mistress of Tugby School, in typical studio pose, *c.* 1900.

Schoolgirls from the Newarke Secondary School, Leicester, April 1911. Back row, left to right: Mabel Martin, Hilda Poyner, -?-, Doris House. Middle row: 'Pompey' Bailey, Ella Hunter, Elsie Mochrie. Front row: Dorothy Humphreys.

Newarke Secondary School hockey team, *c.* 1911.

Some of Sir Bache Cunard's staff at Nevill Holt, photographed by Frederick Hawke of Hallaton, *c.* 1905.

Sometime, about 1900, someone took a snapshot of Mr and Mrs Greening and their son, Nelson. The Leicester directory of 1904 gives only one Greening; Robert, a printer, of 153 Clarendon Park Road.

Eva Lines, of Birstall, *c.* 1913. 'When my sister Eva was twenty one she had a beautiful new dance dress made of a black silk striped material, with a frill round the neck line, and short sleeves, and flounces round the long skirt. These were edged with glittering sequins. I thought she looked beautiful . . . Eva was tall and slim, with classical features, dark brown hair and grey eyes.' (Annie Lines' memories written in 1967).

OUT & ABOUT

'Dinner on the Wherry' was R.C. Stewart's original caption from 1893. The cramped conditions evident in the saloon of the wherry will be recognised by anyone who has 'holidayed' afloat. Stewart's subjects must have held this carefully posed relaxation for several seconds – though how Trevor Jones, caught mid-swig, managed to avoid choking is a mystery!

R.C. Stewart and a party of friends at Swanage, *c.* 1895. Stewart (sitting at the rear of the group) nurses his camera on his lap.

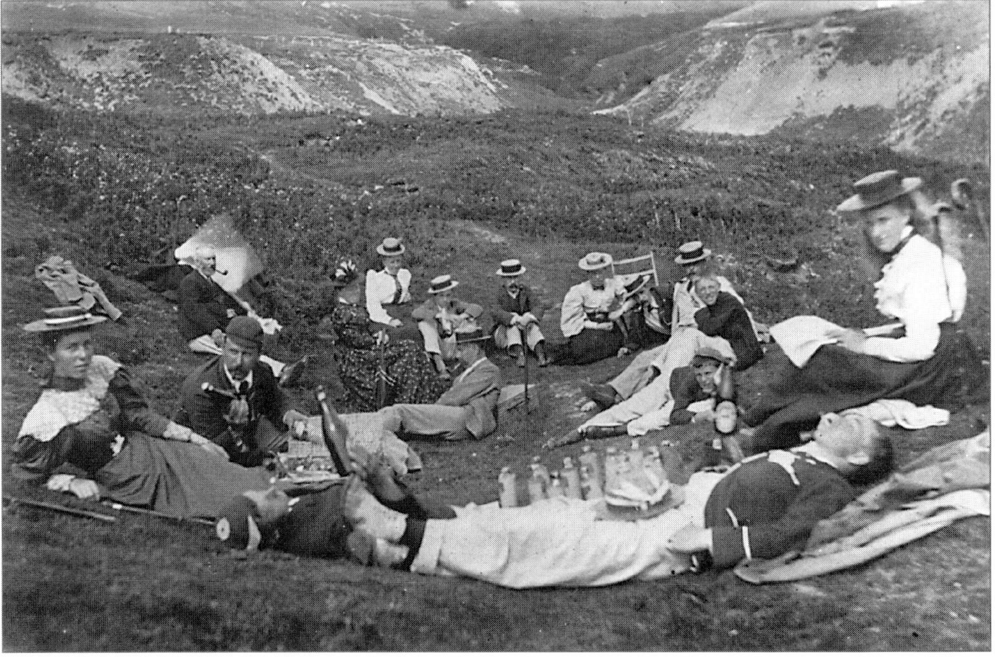

A dozen of ginger beer and a few brown ales later . . . R.C. Stewart and his pals at Swanage, *c.* 1895.

On holiday at Swanage, *c.* 1895. A photograph taken with R.C. Stewart's camera by Mrs Claude Douglas. Then Stewart and Mrs Douglas swapped places.

Mrs Douglas settles beside her husband, the boys at the back hoist their ginger beer bottles and the pipe of the over familiar laddie in the centre goes out and is replaced with a cigarette. The *Church News* remained unread.

Only Mr Polly (H.G. Wells's famous ferryman) is missing! A family crosses the River Trent by the Kings Mill Ferry, Castle Donington, 12 August 1908.

Passengers about to board, at London Road station, *c.* 1910.

This stone gatehouse at Appleby Magna is all that survives of an extensive moated medieval house. The photographer, G.M. Henton, did not record who posed for him when he visited the village one Wednesday in May 1910 but we probably see Frederick Gothard and his family (including his 85-year-old mother, Elizabeth Gothard) lined up outside their home.

Two Hallaton lads take a rest from walking their dog by the Butter Cross, one Wednesday late in September 1910.

The Independent Order of Good Templars gather on the site of the castle in Mountsorrel, *c.* 1910.

Breedon-on-the-Hill, 6 October 1908. The lock-up is visible halfway up the main road through the village.

The Leicester Unemployed Marchers, 1905. Five hundred men, representing four times that number without work in Leicester, took their case to London hoping to deliver an appeal for help to Edward VII.

EVENTS

With his baton under his arm Henry Bramley Ellis leads the Leicester Philharmonic Society in celebration of Queen Victoria's Diamond Jubilee, at the Abbey Park, Leicester, 22 June 1897. Beginning with Mornington's 'Here in cool grot' and Macfarren's 'Up, Up, Ye Dames', the singers proceeded through a succession of glees and part songs to Sir Arthur Sullivan's newly composed 'King of Kings'.

This extraordinary photograph shows the grandstand and crowd at the twelfth Annual Leicester Royal Infirmary Sports, held at Aylestone on Monday 4 July 1892. Held since 1880 in aid of the hospital, the Sports quickly became established as Leicester's most charitable function. Police and Military bands played and a succession of foot and bicycle races were run – or pedalled. The prizes were well worth the exertion : the tea kettle on the right of the table (value £8 6*s*) went to the winner of the 200 yards Flat Handicap while the chiming clock was won by A. Bentley of Leicester who cycled half a mile in just over one minute and ten seconds.

The blurred figures of children fidgeting during the proclamation of Edward VII betray the long exposure time needed to capture the scene at Oakham Castle in January 1901.

Bare-headed (which is odd for Leicester's leading hat and cap manufacturer) and looking particularly puckish, William Wilkins Vincent – for the second time Mayor of Leicester – plants an oak in celebration of George V's coronation, 22 June 1911.

The Labour Party's conference at the Temperance Hall, Leicester in February 1911. J.R. Clynes is on his feet, flanked by Keir Hardie to his left and J. Ramsay MacDonald (who represented Leicester in Parliament from 1906 until 1918) beside the lady to his right. The Rev. F.L. Donaldson, a leader of the Leicester Unemployed March of 1905, sits behind MacDonald's left shoulder.

An unfamiliar sight in bowler hat and spectacles, Kitchener of Khartoum addresses the county's Scouts at the cricket ground, Aylestone, Easter Tuesday 1911.

Lord Kitchener, with the Duke of Rutland in tow, mingles with Leicestershire Scouts.

The Wycliffe Society Motor Car Outing for the Blind, July 1913. A little boy, born without eyes, is helped into one of the Wycliffe Society's cars by Inspector Main of the Leicester Borough police.

Mr Lyent who was unable to hear, see or speak is kept informed through his fingers.

John Murby, a leading light of Leicester's Independent Labour Party, depicted on one of a series of postcards, *c.* 1914.

A strike picket outside Thomas Brown & Co. Ltd's ladies' shoe factory in Humberstone Road, Leicester, *c.* 1912.

Misses Bowker and Pethick on duty outside the Womens Social and Political Union offices at 14 Bowling Green Street, Leicester, *c.* 1914.

Ada Ann Billington, one of a group of suffragettes from Birstall, *c.* 1914.

A sea of straw hats! One of a series of women's suffrage meetings in the Market Place, Leicester, June 1913.

CRIMINALS

Is there a criminal face? The following 'mug-shots' from the Leicester Borough Police may answer the question. The sinister smile above belongs to Louisa McDermott (alias Smith, alias Wilson) who progressed from destitition and reformatory to 3 months gaol for stealing a jacket in 1870, 21 days for obscene language in 1871, 6 months for robbery in 1872, 3 months for assault in 1873, and finally 7 years for shop door robbery in 1874.

William Johnson, alias John Williams (aged 40 in 1873). 'This man frequents race meetings etc. for the purpose of stealing watches and Picking Pockets. . . .'

Mary Ann Brown who was sentenced to 6 months hard labour in May 1877 for two charges of robbery from shops. She was 36 years old.

A flogging at Hull for picking pockets in April 1865 does not seem to have deterred John Lyons. From then until 1874 when he received 3 months hard labour for picking pockets on Leicester Market, Lyons was convicted 5 times more in Hull, and at Durham, York and Manchester. He was still only 19!

The police were advised to keep an eye open for Mary Holgate (alias Green, alias Farrar). Aged 32 in 1875 she was 5 foot 4 inches in height, had light brown hair, blue eyes and a sallow complexion. She was scarred across the nose and on her right jaw. She was 'well known at Wakefield Prison'.

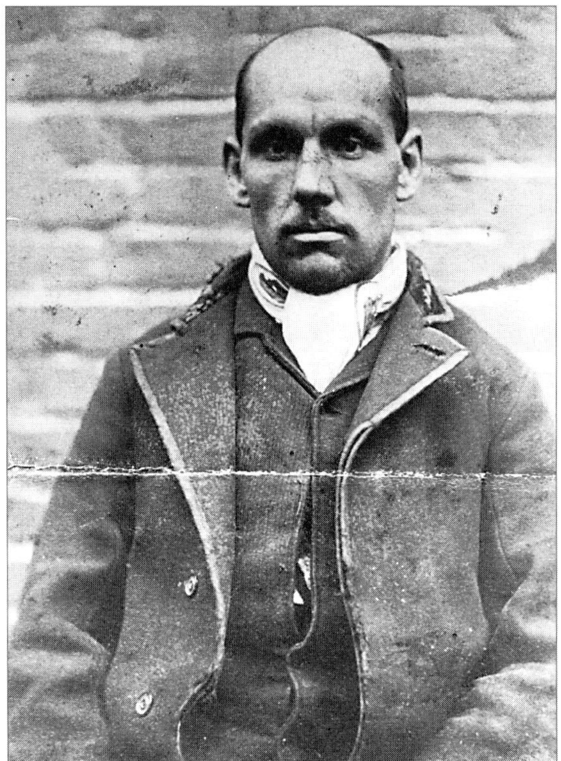

John Brown was convicted at Leicester in January 1876 : 'This man tramped into Leicester too late to lodge at the Union, he walked about the Town a short time, then started out for Birmingham, when he got nearly out of the Town he lifted up a coal cellar Door, got into the House and stole a Gold watch etc., helped himself to something to eat and drink and made his way to Leeds where he was Apprehended when attempting to pledge the watch.'

Crime did not pay George Hamilton. He was arrested in Coventry in January 1875 and sentenced to 12 months hard labour for stealing a watch. He had picked a lady's pocket of £22 in gold the same day – £20 of which his lawyer took for his defence.

'The Duke'. Jacob Boswell was well known to the Leicester police as a card sharper and thief. He was arrested in 1875 and received 6 months hard labour for picking the pockets of passengers in a tram on the way to Leicester Races.

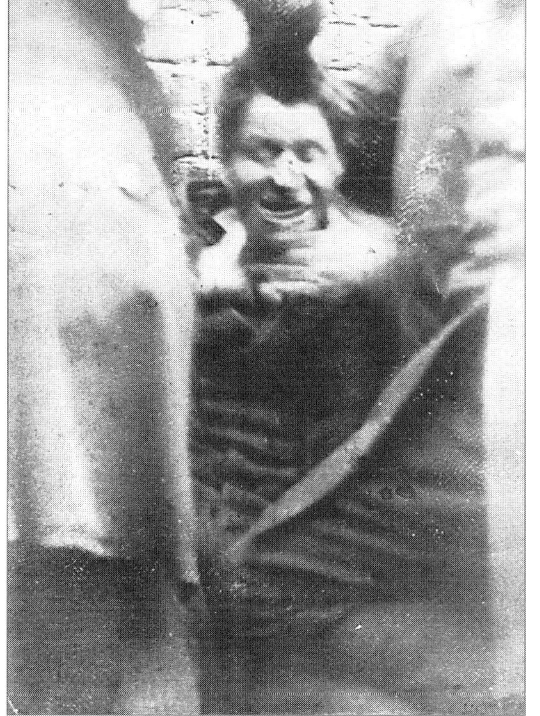

This is John Nichols – the only unwilling subject of a photograph in this book. Nichols was a pick-pocket only recently released from gaol and reluctant to return. The photographer's 'assistants' offering 'reasonable force' are two Leicester Borough policemen.

A *carte-de-visite* photograph of Nemiah Backhouse; a Leicester clerk and bookkeeper with a wife and two children. Perhaps brought down by his fondness for music halls and billiards, Backhouse fled to America to avoid a charge of forgery. Mrs Backhouse presumably provided his likeness for police files.

SECTION FOUR

THE SNAPSHOT (1914 ONWARDS)

The 5*s* Brownie camera of 1900, a simple box with attached cartridge of roll film, revolutionised photography. By the end of the First World War millions of ordinary people could, and did, take photographs. It was the age of the snapshot and millions of 'snaps' were taken – of ordinary people, doing ordinary things.

The professional was still there, though, recording formal occasions, taking portraits and capturing the news. Often still using older technology (cameras with larger negatives for example generally give better images) and working within the privileged confines as the 'official' recorder, the press photographers have left us a remarkable record of Leicestershire people and their activities.

Caught snapping! A photographer recorded at work outside the Town Hall, Leicester, *c.* 1930.

NEWS

The Chief Scout in Leicester, 13 March 1915. The cricket ground was again the scene of a BP Boy Scouts rally (see page 88) this time to greet R.S.S. Baden-Powell himself.

Leicester Royal Navy and Royal Marine reservists drawn up in the Great Central Railway station yard as a guard of honour to greet Admiral of the Fleet Sir David Beatty, 25 July 1919. Beatty's hunting box at Brooksby conferred upon him the status of a 'local'. A popular figure, Beatty had yet to face the criticism of his mishandling of the battle-cruisers at Jutland. Even so he had to share the newspaper front pages with news from the 'Green Bicycle Murder' inquest.

'Yeildeing and payeinge therefore yearlye unto the Mair of the Burrough of Leicester for the time beinge one damaske Rose. . . .' Originally agreed in 1637 this odd rent is still paid by the pub in Loseby Lane, Leicester. Here, in about 1920, the publican, Sydney Smith (?) hands the rose to W. Penn Lewis, the City Treasurer.

Emptying the Trinity Hospital Poor Box, 1928. Harry Hand, the Lord Mayor of Leicester, with his secretary Mr Barsby passes the receipts to the Hospital Matron.

'Fat beast' (so the original caption has it) at the Leicestershire Agricultural Society's annual show, 1 June 1928.

Leicester's 'Shopping Week', 1922. A snip from a pair of golden scissors handed to her by Mr H. Purt, secretary to the Chamber of Commerce and Mrs J.W. Heath, Leicester's Mayoress, declares the city's 'shopping week' open, Saturday 13 May.

An onion shortage in November 1940 led to government price-fixing (at 4½*d* a pound). Onions vanished from the shops except for one 'prominent local store'. The *Leicester Evening Mail* chose not to give the game away and printed only the right half of the picture!

The opening of the County Record Office at 57 New Walk, Leicester on 5 October 1956. Constance and Alfred Halkyard, Leicester's Mayor and Mayoress, with Sir Hilary Jenkinson, late Deputy Keeper of the Public Record Office and the Chairman of the County Council, Sir Robert Martin, examine documents exhibited in celebration of the occasion.

CHARACTERS

Randle & Aspell, auctioneers, sell off materials from the demolished Congregational Chapel, Gallowtree Gate, Leicester, 10 January 1924. It is rare for a photographer to be so helpful to anyone trying to date a picture!

Lt. Col. the Hon. P.C. Evans-Freke 'at ease' at one of the Leicestershire Imperial Yeomanry's annual training camps. Evans-Freke led the Yeomanry's detachment against the Boers in 1900–02 and was killed in the First World War at the head of his regiment at the Battle of Frezenberg in May 1915.

An orphan, with the ribbon of the VC on his chest, William Buckingham returned on leave in the spring of 1916 to the Countesthorpe Cottage Homes where he had lived from 1892 until 1901.

Private William Buckingham VC already wearing three wound stripes, shows Countesthorpe Cottage Homes boys the pay book and field service post cards which saved his life in 1915. (The pay book and cards may be seen at the Leicestershire Record Office.)

'Mobilised'. The same couple we saw married on page 49 we now see ready for service with the St John's Ambulance Brigade.

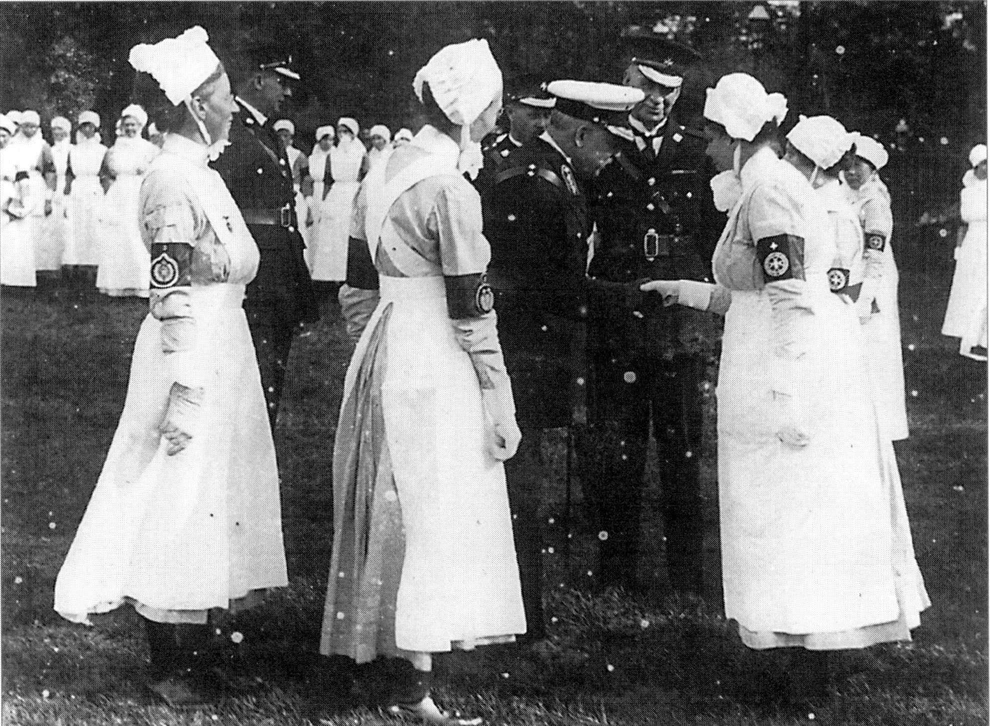

Thanks for a job well done. Senior nurses of the St John's Ambulance receive the congratulations of their chiefs, *c.* 1918.

'Grumpy'! Horace Hodges in costume as 'Grumpy' in his play of the same name, performed at the Royal Opera House, Leicester, September 1918.

Horace Hodges, still in character, on one of his publicity postcards.

The Melton Mowbray photographer Heawood took this picture of 'The Très Jolie Danse Orchestra' in about 1925. The smile and rabbit of the drummer – possibly F. Ward – suggest the trio may have been jollier than they look.

The Board of Wigston Hosiers Ltd, 1920. Back row, left to right: H.A. Spence, T. Carter, T. Gilbert, C. Whyatt, J. Whatton, A. Kirby. Front row: F.A. Smith, H.H. Howkins, S. Kemp, F. Boulter, J.E. Robinson.

A studio portrait of Miss Gertrude Fortescue, of Midland Street, Leicester, *c.* 1930.

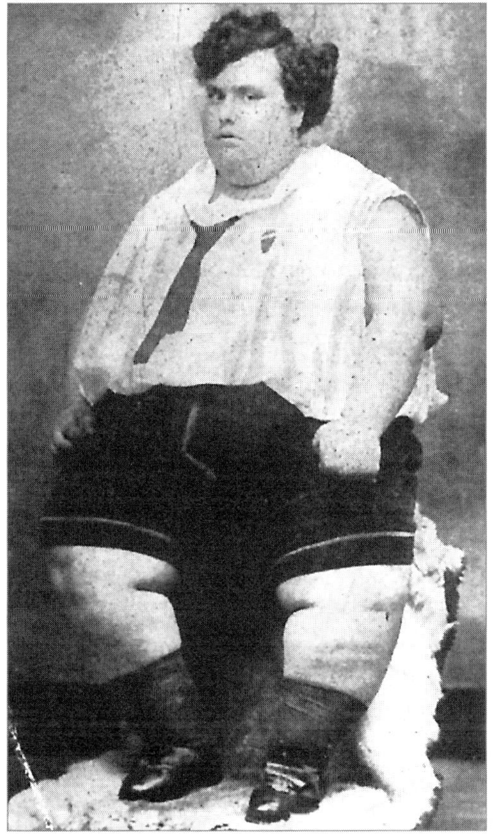

Leonard Mason, famous in the years after the First World War as Leicester's 'fat boy'. He made the best of a melancholy life until his death at the age of 17 at the Islington World Fair of 1920. Only 5 foot 3 inches but weighing 30 stone, Lenny's fate – in a less kindly age perhaps than ours – was to earn money as an exhibit or 'freak'.

W.H. Friswell, known as 'The Colonel', whose eccentric mode of advertising was a feature of Leicester's streets from the early 1920s until his death in 1939.

THE PAGEANT

The Pageant of Leicester City and County held at the Abbey Park, 16–25 June 1932, caused great excitement – and of course the cameras were there!

Leicester One Million Years BC! In one of the shows associated with the Pageant of 1932 some early boy scouts bring home food enough for the entire pack.

Vikings and their captive: players in Leicester's Pageant.

Enter Simon de Montfort. Dr Eric Morrison of Kibworth Beauchamp, as the great Earl of Leicester canters through the 'Newarke Gateway' to open the second scene of Episode Two of the Pageant.

An Historic Committee chaired by Major Guy Paget ensured the accuracy of the Pageant!

A wonderful representation of the Jaws of Hell brought up the rear of the Pentecost Procession from Episode Five of the Pageant. The Guild of St George paraded with their Saint and St Margaret led a dragon across Abbey Park, while William Wyggeston explained plans for his new hospital to Thomas Wyggeston and the mayor.

The forces of darkness – off duty. Demons from the Pentecost procession.

More of Leicester's history from the Pageant. The dying Wolsey portrayed by the Rev. Canon S.T. Winckley, Master of Wyggeston Hospital, supported by the Rev. M.A. Harland and the Rev. S.F. Winckley as Thomas Kingston and William Cavendish respectively.

Elizabethan 'extras' from the Leicester Pageant, 1932.

A Leicester man, dressed as his grandfather might have been to see the opening of Abbey Park fifty years before the Pageant of 1932.

INFORMALITY

Leicester University geographers at the top of Malham Cove, Yorks, *c.* 1950.

'Myself, Skegness, 1921'. A snapshot from the album of Eva M. Smith.

The Smith family of Coningsby House, Aylestone Road, Leicester at Cropston, 12 July 1923. Another snap from Eva's album.

'Group Skegness 1924'. Eva Smith's family on the beach.

'Golfing Skegness 1925'. The Smiths at play. Another of Eva's snapshots.

'Family Group. Skegness'. Elsie and Roy, with Mr and Mrs Smith, snapped by Eva in 1925.

Mr L.E. Dalby, model air-ace, oversees the making of a cup of tea from his mobile canteen, *c.* 1950.

The staff of All Saints' School, Wigston Magna, *c.* 1950. Back row, left to right: H. Herrick, E. Tyler, J.M. Widdowson, Miss Root, P. Tuxford, A.S. Crane, H.(Bob) Baxter. Middle row: Miss Pixton, Mrs Insley, Mrs Parker, Miss Hewes, Miss Daft, Miss Sampson, Miss Rolland, Miss Marvin, Miss Allsopp. Front row: Mrs Harrison, C. Harris.

Leicester's Muriel Road celebrates the coronation of Queen Elizabeth II, 1953.

ACKNOWLEDGEMENTS

The photographs in this book have been drawn, in the main, from the extensive collections of the Leicestershire Museum, Arts and Records Service. Some contemporary photographs are from the author's own collection. The author is grateful to the museum's services photographers, Catherine Lines and Richard Marvin, for their hard work and advice as well as to his colleagues at the Leicestershire Record Office. Especial gratitude must go to Wendy Adams for her customary care in deciphering and typing the manuscript. Thanks are due too to the incumbents of those Leicestershire churches who were so generous and swift to grant permission to reproduce views of tombs and carvings.

Copies of these and many more photographs may be had from the Leicestershire Museums, Arts and Records Service. Enquiries should be made to the Leicestershire Record Office, Long Street, Wigston Magna, Leicester LE18 2AH.

BRITAIN IN OLD PHOTOGRAPHS

erystwyth & North Ceredigion
ound Abingdon
on
erney: A Second Selection
ng the Avon from Stratford to
ewkesbury
rincham
ersham
ound Amesbury
glesey
old & Bestwood
old & Bestwood: A Second
election
ndel & the Arun Valley
bourne
ound Ashby-de-la-Zouch
o Aircraft
esbury
am & Tooting
buryshire
nes, Mortlake & Sheen
nsley
h
consfield
ford
fordshire at Work
worth
erley
ley
eford
ton
ningham Railways
op's Stortford &
wbridgeworth
opstone & Seaford
opstone & Seaford: A Second
election
k Country Aviation
k Country Railways
k Country Road Transport
kburn
kpool
und Blandford Forum
chley
on
rnemouth
dford
ntree & Bocking at Work
on
ntwood
lgwater & the River Parrett
llington
lport & the Bride Valley
erley Hill
hton & Hove
hton & Hove: A Second
election
tol
und Bristol
ton & Norwood
y Broadstairs & St Peters
mley, Keston & Hayes

Buckingham & District
Burford
Bury
Bushbury
Camberwell
Cambridge
Cannock Yesterday & Today
Canterbury: A Second Selection
Castle Combe to Malmesbury
Chadwell Heath
Chard & Ilminster
Chatham Dockyard
Chatham & Gillingham
Cheadle
Cheam & Belmont
Chelmsford
Cheltenham: A Second Selection
Cheltenham at War
Cheltenham in the 1950s
Chepstow & the River Wye
Chesham Yesterday & Today
Cheshire Railways
Chester
Chippenham & Lacock
Chiswick
Chorley & District
Cirencester
Around Cirencester
Clacton-on-Sea
Around Clitheroe
Clwyd Railways
Clydesdale
Colchester
Colchester 1940–70
Colyton & Seaton
The Cornish Coast
Corsham & Box
The North Cotswolds
Coventry: A Second Selection
Around Coventry
Cowes & East Cowes
Crawley New Town
Around Crawley
Crewkerne & the Ham Stone Villages
Cromer
Croydon
Crystal Palace, Penge & Anerley
Darlington
Darlington: A Second Selection
Dawlish & Teignmouth
Deal
Derby
Around Devizes
Devon Aerodromes
East Devon at War
Around Didcot & the Hagbournes
Dorchester
Douglas
Dumfries
Dundee at Work
Durham People

Durham at Work
Ealing & Northfields
East Grinstead
East Ham
Eastbourne
Elgin
Eltham
Ely
Enfield
Around Epsom
Esher
Evesham to Bredon
Exeter
Exmouth & Budleigh Salterton
Fairey Aircraft
Falmouth
Farnborough
Farnham: A Second Selection
Fleetwood
Folkestone: A Second Selection
Folkestone: A Third Selection
The Forest of Dean
Frome
Fulham
Galashiels
Garsington
Around Garstang
Around Gillingham
Gloucester
Gloucester: from the Walwin Collection
North Gloucestershire at War
South Gloucestershire at War
Gosport
Goudhurst to Tenterden
Grantham
Gravesend
Around Gravesham
Around Grays
Great Yarmouth
Great Yarmouth: A Second Selection
Greenwich & Woolwich
Grimsby
Around Grimsby
Grimsby Docks
Gwynedd Railways
Hackney: A Second Selection
Hackney: A Third Selection
From Haldon to Mid-Dartmoor
Hammersmith & Shepherds Bush
Hampstead to Primrose Hill
Harrow & Pinner
Hastings
Hastings: A Second Selection
Haverfordwest
Hayes & West Drayton
Around Haywards Heath
Around Heathfield
Around Heathfield: A Second Selection
Around Helston

Around Henley-on-Thames
Herefordshire
Herne Bay
Heywood
The High Weald
The High Weald: A Second Selection
Around Highworth
Around Highworth & Faringdon
Hitchin
Holderness
Honiton & the Otter Valley
Horsham & District
Houghton-le-Spring & Hetton-le-Hole
Houghton-le-Spring & Hetton-le-Hole: A Second Selection
Huddersfield: A Second Selection
Huddersfield: A Third Selection
Ilford
Ilfracombe
Ipswich: A Second Selection
Islington
Jersey: A Third Selection
Kendal
Kensington & Chelsea
East Kent at War
Keswick & the Central Lakes
Around Keynsham & Saltford
The Changing Face of Keynsham
Kingsbridge
Kingston
Kinver
Kirkby & District
Kirkby Lonsdale
Around Kirkham
Knowle & Dorridge
The Lake Counties at Work
Lancashire
The Lancashire Coast
Lancashire North of the Sands
Lancashire Railways
East Lancashire at War
Around Lancaster
Lancing & Sompting
Around Leamington Spa
Around Leamington Spa: A Second Selection
Leeds in the News
Leeds Road & Rail
Around Leek
Leicester
The Changing Face of Leicester
Leicester at Work
Leicestershire People
Around Leighton Buzzard & Linslade
Letchworth
Lewes
Lewisham & Deptford: A Second Selection
Lichfield

Lincoln
Lincoln Cathedral
The Lincolnshire Coast
Liverpool
Around Llandudno
Around Lochaber
Theatrical London
Around Louth
The Lower Fal Estuary
Lowestoft
Luton
Lympne Airfield
Lytham St Annes
Maidenhead
Around Maidenhead
Around Malvern
Manchester
Manchester Road & Rail
Mansfield
Marlborough: A Second Selection
Marylebone & Paddington
Around Matlock
Melton Mowbray
Around Melksham
The Mendips
Merton & Morden
Middlesbrough
Midsomer Norton & Radstock
Around Mildenhall
Milton Keynes
Minehead
Monmouth & the River Wye
The Nadder Valley
Newark
Around Newark
Newbury
Newport, Isle of Wight
The Norfolk Broads
Norfolk at War
North Fylde
North Lambeth
North Walsham & District
Northallerton
Northampton
Around Norwich
Nottingham 1944–74
The Changing Face of Nottingham
Victorian Nottingham
Nottingham Yesterday & Today
Nuneaton
Around Oakham
Ormskirk & District
Otley & District
Oxford: The University
Oxford Yesterday & Today
Oxfordshire Railways: A Second Selection
Oxfordshire at School
Around Padstow
Pattingham & Wombourne
Penwith
Penzance & Newlyn
Around Pershore
Around Plymouth
Poole
Portsmouth
Poulton-le-Fylde
Preston
Prestwich
Pudsey
Radcliffe
RAF Chivenor
RAF Cosford
RAF Hawkinge
RAF Manston
RAF Manston: A Second Selection
RAF St Mawgan
RAF Tangmere
Ramsgate & Thanet Life
Reading
Reading: A Second Selection
Redditch & the Needle District
Redditch: A Second Selection
Richmond, Surrey
Rickmansworth
Around Ripley
The River Soar
Romney Marsh
Romney Marsh: A Second Selection
Rossendale
Around Rotherham
Rugby
Around Rugeley
Ruislip
Around Ryde
St Albans
St Andrews
Salford
Salisbury
Salisbury: A Second Selection
Salisbury: A Third Selection
Around Salisbury
Sandhurst & Crowthorne
Sandown & Shanklin
Sandwich
Scarborough
Scunthorpe
Seaton, Lyme Regis & Axminster
Around Seaton & Sidmouth
Sedgley & District
The Severn Vale
Sherwood Forest
Shrewsbury
Shrewsbury: A Second Selection
Shropshire Railways
Skegness
Around Skegness
Skipton & the Dales
Around Slough
Smethwick
Somerton & Langport
Southampton
Southend-on-Sea
Southport
Southwark
Southwell
Southwold to Aldeburgh
Stafford
Around Stafford
Staffordshire Railways
Around Staveley
Stepney
Stevenage
The History of Stilton Cheese
Stoke-on-Trent
Stoke Newington
Stonehouse to Painswick
Around Stony Stratford
Around Stony Stratford: A Second Selection
Stowmarket
Streatham
Stroud & the Five Valleys
Stroud & the Five Valleys: A Second Selection
Stroud's Golden Valley
The Stroudwater and Thames & Severn Canals
The Stroudwater and Thames & Severn Canals: A Second Selection
Suffolk at Work
Suffolk at Work: A Second Selection
The Heart of Suffolk
Sunderland
Sutton
Swansea
Swindon: A Third Selection
Swindon: A Fifth Selection
Around Tamworth
Taunton
Around Taunton
Teesdale
Teesdale: A Second Selection
Tenbury Wells
Around Tettenhall & Codshall
Tewkesbury & the Vale of Gloucester
Thame to Watlington
Around Thatcham
Around Thirsk
Thornbury to Berkeley
Tipton
Around Tonbridge
Trowbridge
Around Truro
TT Races
Tunbridge Wells
Tunbridge Wells: A Second Selection
Twickenham
Uley, Dursley & Cam
The Upper Fal
The Upper Tywi Valley
Uxbridge, Hillingdon & Cowley
The Vale of Belvoir
The Vale of Conway
Ventnor
Wakefield
Wallingford
Walsall
Waltham Abbey
Wandsworth at War
Wantage, Faringdon & the Vale Villages
Around Warwick
Weardale
Weardale: A Second Selection
Wednesbury
Wells
Welshpool
West Bromwich
West Wight
Weston-super-Mare
Around Weston-super-Mare
Weymouth & Portland
Around Wheatley
Around Whetstone
Whitchurch to Market Drayton
Around Whitstable
Wigton & the Solway Plain
Willesden
Around Wilton
Wimbledon
Around Windsor
Wingham, Addisham & Littlebourne
Wisbech
Witham & District
Witney
Around Witney
The Witney District
Wokingham
Around Woodbridge
Around Woodstock
Woolwich
Woolwich Royal Arsenal
Around Wootton Bassett, Cricklade & Purton
Worcester
Worcester in a Day
Around Worcester
Worcestershire at Work
Around Worthing
Wotton-under-Edge to Chipping Sodbury
Wymondham & Attleborough
The Yorkshire Wolds

To order any of these titles please telephone our distributor, Littlehampton Book Services on 01903 72159
For a catalogue of these and our other titles please ring Regina Schinner on 01453 731114